HOW THE PAIN OF HEARTBREAK PROPELLED ME TO HEALING

HOW THE PAIN OF HEARTBREAK PROPELLED ME TO HEALING

7 STAGES YOU NEED TO KNOW IN ORDER TO HEAL... IGNORANCE OF CHAPTER 5 WILL PARALYZE THE PROCESS

ARNOLD AUSTIN

Arnold Austin
How the pain of heartbreak propelled me to healing
7 stages you need to know in order to heal... ignorance of chapter 5 will paralyze the process

Published by Spines Publishing Platform
ISBN: 979-8-89691-102-9

CONTENTS

CHAPTER 1

The story started on January 12th, 1992. This is the day I made a commitment to my then-wife that I would love, honor, and cherish her, leave all others, and cleave to her. At some point, from that day to December 4th, 2016, something must have changed. I wasn't fully aware of it, and why I said something changed was because that night was the beginning of numerous nights where I dreamed that me and my now ex-wife would be getting a divorce.

The thing with dreams that I'm given is that they are real. They are emotional—I cry in them, I laugh, and I'm clear on what's happening while I'm asleep. The part that confused me about the dream was that I didn't think the difficulties we had at the moment in our marriage warranted a divorce. So, I was confused. What I ended up doing was that upon waking up and because of the raw pain i felt i went into prayer i cried out to God desiring answers once i was done in prayer i talked to my wife and revealed to her everything that i had just seen because i was trying anything i could to get answers which was difficult with my wife because she would normally shut down in any conversation that dealt with serious vulnerable issues but she talked about this with me and she reassured me that it had to be someone elsa and that we were fine -- She would tell me what I wanted to hear to reassure me everything was good, that it was probably someone else, and after that i I would pray about it and fast, asking for clarity and saying, *If it is us, can You change Your mind, Most High? What can we do to turn this around?*

Over a period of time, the dreams changed from showing us getting divorced and then it started being shown different sexual acts of betrayal, financial deception, and some type of dark magic. Even as I was shown later, around 2022, to stop eating her food because she had been controlling me with substances she had put into my food. The dark substances that were being used and the secret practices she had been doing had placed blindness and ignorance on me, and it wasn't until I saw. By the end of the year 2021, I was asking if I was supposed to stay with my now ex-wife. Because it was revealed to me that there was information about her that would come out, and it was going to be extremely hurtful and painful, bringing shame and embarrassment to my family and our name. There were even videos out there.

I started really trying to figure out what to do with this information. This wasn't any information that I had revealed to anyone, and I had known it since 2016, so I had held on to this information for approximately five years. In that process of time, I was hoping that God would turn things around and that she would just open up and explain to me what was going on. But all that I got from her was deception and manipulation. Through this process, I didn't say anything to anyone because I was ashamed, confused, and I was hurt. To think that you have dedicated yourself, life, health, support, and love to someone, and all you get back is distance and pretense.

In public, the goal always appeared like she was so nice and so caring, someone who was supportive—that was all part of the act or part of a role she was playing, but it was always for an outward showing in public for other people. But at home, it was the opposite, a different story; you received a lot of the manipulation. The thing I learned later was that she was an expert at using your strengths and weaknesses against you.

When I had that final dream at the end of 2022 about all of the shame that was going to be revealed, and that was coming out, that's when I was ready to get out. By chance, I was given a confirmation to leave in one of the strangest ways ever. At this time, I was doing a lot of meditation and praying. There was one morning, when I woke up and part of the dream, I heard that I should reach out to one of my sister's friends, whose name was Shan. I had only met her three times previously and had only spoken casual greetings like, "Hi, how are you? Nice to meet you," and things similar to that. So, because I didn't know Shan, I reached out to my sister to see if I could get her contact information. When I reached out to my sister Pam, she revealed to me that Shan was running a healing community online. So, based on that and getting her phone number, I reached out.

When I did, initially, we were playing phone tag, but once we spoke, I felt like I was supposed to hire her as a coach to help me start my online business. That was my initial perception of why I was supposed to get in contact with her. On about our third or fourth conversation, we were talking as usual, then she got quiet, and she began to say, "Arnold, don't take this as if it's strange or weird, but your grandmother keeps running in front of me, waving her arms and hands trying to get my attention." After she said this, she began to explain to me that she had had a near-death experience and because of it, she sees people's loved ones from time to time who have passed away, and after that, she was used. But my grandmother, who died or transitioned in 1992, revealed that my spouse had performed many betrayals over the years. "Right now, you have to get out." As she was talking, based on the fact I've only met her a few times in person, the talks we had were strictly business; the times we met on Zoom, I was blown away at the clear, precise answers to questions I was getting because there is no way that she should have known what I was writing in my dream book and what I was praying and asking God about. This is the point when the real pain started, and even after this, it took me months to actually start filing for divorce.

Numerous other examples of people appeared in my life and told me of things that they knew that had been going on behind my back. One just so happened to be an individual who lived near a flip that I had finished, and this neighbor revealed certain behavior that she noticed and how my Audi and another car would meet over there all the time. But you could tell that it wasn't for a house showing because it was the same two people every time, and there were too many synchronicities at that time. But through all of this, this is how my life of eventual service to others would be initiated. When you spend any amount of years with a person, and you commit your heart to them, then they turn around and betray you, and after betrayal, lie to you, then go into the community and spread lies about you, and then try to present themselves as being a great spouse and how much support and help they were the whole time—because of ignorance and not listening to the internal voice, ignoring what my gut was saying—this experience has taught me to hear, feel, and obey my intuition. My suffering was a direct result of not hearing, not understanding, and not obeying the voice of God. My desire is to be in alignment with God's word. You can suffer, thinking it will get better, but you will eventually have to do what I had to do, which was accepting what I was being shown for 5 years. As I look back, I know it was well beyond five years. I had to stop ignoring the voice of God within me and using scriptures and Biblical verses to condone things that I didn't want to accept, which was very challenging and difficult. This is where I really discovered the true level of intuition that I had, and through this healing journey, I would have to go back and heal my intuition.

One of the biggest mistakes that I made continually, over and over, was I would be shown something spiritually—whether through a dream, just having a knowing, or through a gut feeling—and I would ask my then-wife about it. Because she was in the energy of manipulation and deception, it was ignorant for me to think that she would be able to tell me the truth. It was easy for me to be manipulated because I had already deceived myself based on an image of who I thought she was, based upon what she said. Even though her actions didn't match what she said at that time, until the end of 2022, I would still argue and debate against myself.

It was then that I finally realized who and what she was: an immature woman with bad communication skills who was emotionally unintelligent, not available physically or emotionally, and who considered any conversation about our relationship an argument, even though it was a discussion. At some point, I just felt exhausted and tired of trying.

I was tired of all of the pretense that she would put on in front of others, but I couldn't get any results at home. It was when I started accepting these things that my true spiritual awakening began, but also, that's where the real pain started. Needless to say, there was a lot of behavior that, once I was away from her, I could see clearly.

After our divorce on February 15th, 2023, I now understand why she shut down every conversation, didn't want to discuss anything, and always accused me of arguing. All I wanted was for us to try and communicate to see if there was a resolution or solution, but I was met with stonewalling and roadblocks.

At this point in writing, I am grateful for all of the events that have taken place. It was and will be, the springboard to my new and bright future because everything truly has worked together for my benefit. It was at this point that I realized that I had been in a state of shock because I struggled with still believing all of the things I was seeing. I am still being made aware that the secrets done behind my back are still coming out.

When we went through the divorce, she acted like God had revealed to her not to fight me on it but just give me what I wanted. But the truth was that she was excited to get her new undercover relationship started, and I was okay with it—I just needed to feel peace. Because at this point, I didn't realize I had started the grieving process because of loss. One of the keys to loss was that I learned to no longer believe anything that she said because her words of affirmation and love did not match her behavior. At this point, being exhausted mentally, I wanted to be left alone and go somewhere alone. It didn't matter to me about the smear campaign and all of the negative things that were being said.

I was amazed, though, how they mobilized many portions of my family—one of my sisters and various other people and families that went to my dad's church, as well as a lot of mutual contacts. The sad thing about all of this is that many of these people made decisions based on hearing one side of a story. Whenever you make a decision based on one side of one story, you're always going to make a bad decision because you cannot make an intelligent decision with partial information; you can only make an uninformed decision.

But through it, I learned the difference between those who love me and those who don't, those who support me and those who won't, and what a relative is versus a family member. Also, what happened in this process is that I was isolated because of the smear campaign, which was a blessing in disguise. What it made me do was fall back on what I was doing anyway, which was prayer. It caused me to lay on my face and cry out to God for help, for strength, for courage, for the ability to keep fighting, and that He would remove the heavy weight of the pain and heartbreak from my heart and that my soul would be renewed.

When you are completely alone, prayer is the solution. I'm grateful to God for my mom and dad because I had them. But the only issue was my dad was in recovery from having a recent stroke, so there was a part of me that felt a sense of guilt in trying to rely on them in this time frame.

It wasn't until one day, in meditation, that I was shown that I had to stay connected to my mom, which was important because I was blessed with a mother full of wisdom—the type of wisdom where she doesn't make decisions based on her emotions. When I would go and have conversations with my mom, she would often just listen to the things that I was saying—not interjecting, not saying anything. She would listen, she would ask me questions, and we would pray together, which was a powerful blessing.

I was blessed with a nephew and a son who would reach out periodically. They would text me saying something like, *"Yo Unc,"* or *"Yo Dad, you good?"* It makes me laugh now when I think about it, but during that time frame, I needed a little help, and many times it came at a critical moment.

If you are in the process of a loss, know for a fact that grief will be a byproduct of the loss. The loss is what causes the grief. Healing through grief is a process of ups and downs, good days and bad days. I'd like to encourage you to keep your head up. Just take it one day at a time, sit in it, feel it, and allow yourself to surrender to the process.

There is no set amount of time it takes to heal. The key is just to heal.

This experience has made me stronger and more determined to fulfill the true purpose of my existence on this Earth, which is to help individuals heal from heartbreak and, in the process, help them discover their God-given purpose and fulfill their destiny.

The reason I didn't tell my side of the story then, and I'm telling it now, is because I wanted to protect my sons. The second reason was I was shown that it wasn't the right time to tell my side of the story and what happened. Symbolically, it was me being willing to fall on the sword for them, which was difficult but necessary at that time. Through that decision and the obedience connected to it, there were certain consequences that came with it.

One of the consequences, which is pretty well known, is that generally when there is a divorce, most men lose contact with their kids or grandkids within one year after the divorce because of maybe the moving challenges or just other life events that take place or come up.It was difficult to think that the reason for the divorce was based upon her action but she was rewarded with our kids and grandkids visiting her and i was alone but i had to accept it as a consequence

The reason I knew that I personally needed to move on and go towards the avenue of healing was because I didn't want to become the typical angry person—the angry person who never addresses what they felt, the angry person who never deals with what they just experienced. I knew that if I didn't address this personally, it would have affected me emotionally as well as physically.

Either we will become the disciples of destruction, or we will be people of love, going through and finding our way—even if we have to do it alone. Pain in life is inevitable, but suffering is optional. How long do you want to suffer with that pain?

I'm writing this book because one of the tools that I found through this time alone was writing. It was easy for me to fall back on because I wasn't telling a story to anyone; writing became an outlet. It was therapeutic—a way of getting out of my heart what I was feeling.

Be honest with what you're feeling and what you're thinking. You will go through a stage where you're blaming others, but at some point through the journey, when your focus leaves other people, and you really start taking a real deep introspection and looking at yourself, you'll see that there were things within you, as well as within them, that needed to change.

There are things in them, as well as in you, that could have been better. At the end of the day, you both made the decision to be in a relationship together. This is why I don't believe in it being one person's fault, because a relationship involves two people.

One of the keys to having success is not allowing third parties or other people to come into your relationship, to protect it, honor it, love it, and cherish it.

One of the personal revelations that I had to look at myself through the examination process and reveal was that I didn't take the time to even study the essence of those words before making a decision to get married. Many people you meet today and every other day are getting married. I would suggest that you take the time to actually study and look up what it means to honor your person, what it means to cherish your person, and what it means to love your person.

Your idea of love could be different from theirs. If you've never had a conversation about it—if you've never had an in-depth thought about what it means to them and what they think it means to you—there will be a breakdown at some point throughout the relationship because the two people who are supposed to be joined together are now being pulled apart.

The important key to healing is that it can be done in a group, but it is an individual, personal event. You must focus on yourself and not look at anyone else, especially your ex. The love, consideration, and patience that you invested in them—it's time to take that energy back and see the value within yourself. You are fearfully and wonderfully made, and I believe in you. I see your success on your healing journey.

Some initial lessons that are magnified through this process are: you will be able to identify family versus relatives; you will also know what manipulation looks like; you will also pay closer attention to individuals' actions versus their words. You will understand self-love from this point on by setting healthy boundaries between things that you will allow and things that you won't. You will consider yourself in every event that should take place from this point forward. You will have a clearer vision of what you will and what you won't allow. You'll be clear on what you want based on experiencing what you didn't want. You'll increase your self-image and your independence and know that there is nothing that can stop you from this point forward.

The first stage that happens to individuals in loss and grief is shock. The stages that I'm going to share with you are all stages that I went through as I was on the healing journey. I was fortunate that, through meditation, it was revealed to me what was going on in me, and so I made a decision that I would document this process so that I can help to show individuals how they can heal and grow from their difficulties.

There is a possibility of healing your heart and staying on the winning side of love, joy, peace, gratitude, and abundance, as well as having a heart that is still open and pliable. The other alternative is hate, lies, deceit, malice, vengeance, and also having a hard heart full of bitterness by not healing. This choice was a no-brainer for me. I choose healing, and I reject becoming a disciple of destruction.

2. COURAGE

Courage doesn't represent the absence of fear but the ability to follow through with the task at hand regardless of how you feel and what others think healing is. It is a challenging direction to go towards because it requires an in-depth look into ourselves and honesty about the things that have to change in order for us to become better. It is the only and best way to go. If we choose to other direction the path of least resistance, that's the path of denial of a healing that is needed; and not examining ourselves but putting all of the blame on others.Of course, that would not allow for any accountability to be taken. But it is the path of least resistance, and being stuck and stagnant, and staying where we are, repeating the same cycles until we are willing to address, from an honest place, what has happened and what can we do to rectify it so we can move on with our lives. Courage will be required for healing. The fact that you're reading this book is courage. The fact that you were able to leave that abusive relationship is courage. The fact that you were able to leave that long-term relationship is courage. The fact that you don't have all the answers but are moving on is courage. You fighting for what's right against those that are opposing you without just a cause it's courage. You standing alone in truth as you are being lied on and ostracized is courage. You leaving and not having a place to go is courage. But because you are in a dangerous environment and you have no other alternative, and for your safety to leave is courageous, especially if you have children involved. You are willing to leave false security for uncertainty so that you can access safety. Some instances of courage are based upon internal motivation, and other times it can be an external environment that triggered the move.

 Fear is a reaction; courage is a decision

 Knowing when to walk away is wisdom; being able to is courage; walking away with your head held high is dignity.

A story comes to mind of a client from my past who was in an abusive, toxic, and violent relationship. After she left, she was in another state, hidden and on her healing path. I asked her about the process of leaving that relationship, and she said that one of the most difficult things that you could do when you're in these toxic relationships is leaving, because you are risking your life. If you leave you're risking your life and if you stay you're risking your life.

Some may think that it's love if you stay in these relationships, but what it actually represents is a bond a toxic bond or trauma bond which represents that you are bonded to this person by some form of trauma that both parties can relate to or are In need of healing from. At some point, this client that I'll call Simone understood that this wasn't love

that was keeping her there; it was fear; it was torment; it was codependency that was keeping her there, so when she decided that she needed to leave, she had to put together a plan that involved getting her spouse arrested and sent to jail, but also going to court and following up on upholding the sentence that was given and also moving to another state

to start her healing journey. Her story is a story that many have lived and they were not able to make it out. It cost them the ultimate price which was their life. So for her to make the decision to leave was a powerful example of courage.

> Fear is a reaction, but courage is a decision. Make the decision today to take courage with you. Joshua, who was the predecessor of Moses in the biblical example, was commanded to be strong and of great courage. As part of the requirement, he needed to apply to receive the promises that were given to him and the children of Israel. He had to take courage and strength to do what needed to be done.

One of the things that I found to be true in my own life that in order to get what I wanted, I needed to make the first step. I always needed to do something outside of my comfort level to get to the next level in life. When your focus is on the goal or the objective that you want to achieve, then taking action and doing the work is a natural byproduct or result, because the desire that you want needs to be greater than Where You Are in this present state of lack of unfulfilled potential or unfulfilled promises.

The first thing that you need to know is what it is that you want. Do you want to continue in this toxic, unhealthy, codependent, violent, narcissistic relationship, or are you tired? Have you had enough? Are you ready to experience the other side of life? If you want a new side of life urgently enough, you will take with you courage, which will exemplify the epitome of strength. It is important that you recognize that you are courageous. Just the thought of you going through all of the difficulties you have endured, but yet you're still standing. You're moving away to an area you don't know, starting out new again, which mentally can be overwhelming. But look at you—you're doing it, in fear but with elegance, strength, and grace.

You need to celebrate yourself, in order to leave someone that you loved and wanted, but you know that the relationship isn't of any benefit or good for you and is destroying you. It's pulling you down to low levels and even with that said, many individuals are not strong enough to leave. So they'll stay and endure more trauma and abuse because of the unspoken *bond* that they have with the individual. This bond has to be severed so that they can move on, grow, and evolve—like you are—to become the fullness of the person that they are destined to be.

FOUR STAGES OF THE
COURAGE WHEEL

*S*tage 1 of the courage wheel, that you will need to read, is something; hearing something or seeing something, maybe on social media, maybe a news program, a television show, a documentary, or word of mouth from a friend or family member. But the bottom line is that you will need to learn something and what happens when we learn something that we don't know? Often it will lead to getting motivated or inspired. This is a great start for you tackling the task at hand. Motivation is the key, whether it's intrinsic or extrinsic. Based on the information we receive, it will ignite a sense that there's something else possible for us, which will take us to Stage 2 of the courage wheel.

Once we hear and a sense of belief is created, that is how faith and trust in what was said are activated. When this happens, you will be encouraged to do something. This is where Stage 3—courage—is introduced because your courage isn't based on what you have or who you are; it is based on the desire that was created when you learned that new information that inspired you and as a result motivated you. This is why you're at the stage of Courage because you also believed what you heard, and enough faith was injected into your system to believe that, "Maybe this is possible." Even with that being said, with courage, you still may be afraid and unsure. And again, the desire: how important is it to you? What are you willing to give up, to sacrifice, to go without? What are you willing to rest? When we are set in stone and fixed on the objective, then the next step is Step 4: action.

When everything that we have discussed from 1 to 3 has happened—when we've learned the new information, heard it, and it has created a level of belief and trust in this—and because we trusted, we were courageous enough to take action. These stages can happen instantaneously over a very short period of time. This isn't something that takes a long time to do. It's all based upon us learning, hearing, believing, trusting, and then taking action and doing. But the true sign of Courage is taking action, regardless of how uncomfortable you are with the task. It's just being willing to do what needs to be done and believing it will work in your favor.

There's a tremendous lesson that we all can learn from the parable of the cow and the buffalo. It is said that when a storm is coming, the cow will run with the storm, in the same direction that the storm is coming, but the buffalo will run the opposite direction, into the face of the storm. What they find is that the buffalo will spend less time in the storm because of the courage to face the challenge and to go forward regardless. But the cow, because of running along with the storm, stays in that storm over extended long periods of time. Because they didn't meet the storm head-on but ran with it, they stay much longer in the suffering and in the storm.

So, what we can learn from this parable is that when we can face our difficulties, when we can embrace courage, when we can embrace the fear of taking action, but take action regardless, then we exemplify the same courage of the example of the Buffalo. Because they are running headfirst into the incoming storm, understanding that the storm will be difficult, but it will be only for a short period of time. Face your storm, believing that everything is working together for your benefit.

Take time now to write in your journal about courage and ways that you have been courageous concerning your healing, concerning your relationship, and in your life concerning your occupation. What does courage mean to you? How can you exemplify more courage? If you haven't seen examples of courage, how can you be an example of courage to those loved ones around you?

As you write in your journal, write about the struggle of being courageous, write about your fears, write about your apprehensions. Once you're done writing for today, because part of your healing journey—which will be beneficial to you in an extreme help—is taking the time every day to write about your day, the events that have transpired, whether they were positive in nature or negative. Write about how you felt emotionally" if you were heartbroken, if you were emotional today, if you were angry today. What did you feel? Why did you feel it? Why were you triggered? And changes that you see that can be made? I encourage you to do this daily because it will allow you to see patterns over a period of time.

3. SHOCK

If you are reading or listening to this book, there was a series of events that called you to action, and the igniting of your next moves in life were triggered by the events that probably caused shame and hurt. I used the word "shame," it was the word that was given to me in a dream, which concerned the behavior of my now ex-wife. At the time, I was shown that she was doing things that would cause shame, extreme hurt, and embarrassment to me and to our family, and that I would be in pain because of it. Later on, before our marriage ended, I found out about her being in adulterous affairs and that she had been doing different things with money from my business account, moving it to other places. Also, she was putting things in my food and water to control me and to also make me sick. And, as uncomfortable as I am to talk about this, the agenda was to ultimately eliminate me from all this 3D reality. But through all of it, I was protected spiritually without knowing I needed protection.

The topic for chapter 2 is "shock." In the midst of finding out about all of these betrayals, I was in extreme heartbreak. One of the parts about heartbreak that is so challenging is where it originated—it comes from familiar friends, family, loved ones, and those that you have invested the completeness of your heart. They are the ones that can and may hurt you. So now, what do you do with this pain? This is a level of pain that has caused many to go into rages of anger and do violent acts. The thing with hurt is it's something that all of us handle in different ways, based on our emotional intelligence, environment, and the state of mind I discovered later.

As I started finding out what were some of the things that happened, I realized that I was in a state of shock when I first discovered things that had been going on behind my back for years. I was hurt, I felt betrayed, deceived, and I know now that I was in a state of shock because I couldn't wrap my mind around the fact or believe what I knew to be the absolute truth. I felt in a daze mentally. I fell out of touch with reality, and I remember that I kept saying over and over, "I can't believe this. I can't believe this. I can't believe this. I can't believe that she would do this." I was partially saying this because the new information that was being introduced about my then-relationship didn't align with the image or information I had in my mind about her. So, my mind was in a mental battle. I was really unclear and indecisive, which is not like me.

This is a poem that I read that made a tremendous impression on me, and it said: "The shock is too great; our minds protect us by only allowing the reality to seep in slowly over time, as much loss as we can manage in that moment." This is such a blessing, just more confirmation as of how wonderfully we have been made and how our bodies are self-healing. We innately have a way of protecting and defending ourselves, and shock is one of those powerful tools in our tool shed. It allows us to gradual process of grasping what has happened. Even though you are in shock, there is a pertinent decision that needs your attention, and that would be you making the decision after finding out about all of the betrayals and the deception. Even though it's painful emotionally, physically, and psychologically, you have to decide between two roads. One road is the road of least resistance: it's the road where you don't ever forgive, heal, or do any introspection. It's a road paved and excuses and blame, pointing the finger at others. It's also the road that aligns us to become disciples of *destruction*.

I called this "Disciples of Destruction" because if you don't heal from the pain, many times you will go out and meet new individuals, perpetuating the pain we felt by keeping up our guards up as high as possible and inflicting pain and trauma upon unsuspecting victims. Again, if now after this happens to them, if they don't heal but instead continue down a path of Destruction until someone decides to say "enough" and they decide that maybe there is another way. That other way is the most beneficial to you: to go through the healing, to go on the *journey* of self-reflection and self-evaluation, looking at ways you can grow and move on from the pain, and how the pain over a period of time is part of your process of growth and expansion and developing, because when you actually forgive, can still be loving, and release blame and criticism, you will free yourself from holding on to negative emotions.

This is important because trauma that happens in our lives, if we don't release it do prayer through meditation, through journaling, or releasing ceremonies to forgiveness; the trauma will hold in your body—in one of your organs. Eventually, over a period of time, it will cause sickness and disease because of the unresolved issues and trauma. And because of the pain not being removed and being replaced with forgiveness and love, and freely moving on with your life. Knowing that every person that comes into our lives is part of a lesson that you need to learn so that you can grow. This is one of the most important decisions that you will make, and many times the decision isn't something you sit down and talk about to yourself. But through this journey, I became aware that there are four stages of shock. Before my particular life experience, I was fortunate enough to not get into some of the more severe stages, which can cause serious health issues.

Many individuals that go to heartache are in a State of Shock, which could be considered an initial stage. Because the issue of heartbreak is an emotional issue, which also has physical elements of trauma, but a vehicle accident or shooting of some sort of some caliber has more of a physical element, with possible smaller portions affecting mentally. Some of the signs that you may have been in shock are the fact that you were light-headed, dizzy, foggy, and unclear; that's part of the process of your blood not circulating fully while you were in shock.

One way that I could identify that I was in shock later on, as I was in pursuit of my healing, was when I recall saying often that "I can't believe that this is happening" or "Why has this happened to me?" Why it was so difficult it's because, up to that point, I hadn't had a mind that was open enough to see or believe what I was shown or seeing. I found out later that my now-ex was using spell rituals and putting things in my food to keep me stuck in the view I had of her, which was a portrait that I had drawn of her in our early stages of meeting. And now the behavior I was seeing wasn't matching what I believed about her.

Yet again, I would make the cardinal mistake that, if you are reading or listening, I hope you never make, and that's to question or ask your person, "Are they being faithful or are they cheating?" Just remember, if they are being unfaithful, the secret of the affair, the running around, the secret calls, all the planning hiding, is deceit and a critical part of feeling their diet, fueling their diabolical plan. So, you, many times, aren't going to get an admission of guilt. As a matter of fact, you will get a strong conviction and stance of their innocence, and eventually, it will be turned around on you.

They will go into operation DARVO. The psychology field has come up with an acronym to describe the behavior that is displayed by master manipulators and deceptive gaslighters. The D in Darvo stands for *Denial.* The A stands for *Attack.* The R stands for *Reverse,* this is where they will reverse and shift the blame on you by accusing you of being jealous, insecure, or accusing you of some behavior. Because the next acronym is the V which stands for *Victim*. They will make themselves the victim, so if you start defending yourself based on them accusing you of something that you know you didn't do and they know that you didn't do but it's part of the manipulating process to get you to stop talking about them and start defending yourself. The O stands for *Offender*. Now, you will be the offender. They will push all of the blame on you. You are the reason for whatever infraction they brought up. It has something to do with you, or something that you said, or something that you did in the past. All of this started by you wanting to get clarity about something you saw, whether it was a text, a dream, a conversation, or a call that you overheard. Whatever it was doesn't matter right now.

The most critical point that you need to grasp and hold on to is that they are an enemy of *deceit* and lies. If they are cheating, anything that you question or ask them, you are going to get an untruthful, deceptive answer. You can't expect truth from a lie. They show you that they are in this energy. Believe in it and save yourself a lot of pain by not trusting anything that comes out of their mouth. James Brown had a song, and in the song, he said, "They're talking loud but they're saying nothing."

Say this with me out loud five times: **"I am in perfect alignment with all people, places, and things that are a part of a positive benefit."**

Say this also five times out loud: **"I am grateful and thankful that I am in alignment with positive people with pure hearts and good intentions for me."**

Go follow Arnold Austin on youtube; https://www.youtube.com/channel/UCBHsTrBoLNDIzbEh8oTtVeg

To gain access tour exclusive private healing community click the link: http://www.skool.com/healing-hearts-community-3442

4. DENIAL

enial represents that you don't want to accept that something is true. Earlier, I spoke about the struggle of accepting that my spouse was unfaithful in our 30-year marriage, and also she was involved with deceptive, harmful, and hurtful financial activities against myself and our children. I refused to accept the truth, because the truth was revealed to me in numerous dreams over the years that we were married, but I refused to accept what I was saying. I realized later that I was being unjust in my judgment of my ex-wife being deceptive and untruthful when I realized that I was gaslighting and being untruthful to myself because I refused to accept the things that I was seeing. Instead, often, I was making excuses for what I was seeing, and generally, it was based upon my religious beliefs—because of not wanting to judge others, to love your fellow man, to encourage others, to be a support—things like that.

In order to gaslight yourself, you have to lie to yourself concerning the thing that you're seeing—that it is not true. The difference between lying to someone and gaslighting is that if someone is lying, and you bring them proof of their activities and of the things they've done, generally, they'll admit it at that point. But a gaslighter, regardless of if you have video proof, email proof, or you saw him with your own eyes, will lie and hold on to denying that what you saw is true. Generally, this is where that DARVO technique, that I mentioned in the earlier chapter, comes into play: they will deny, accuse, and reverse to make themselves the victim, and then you'll be defending yourself.

One of the biggest challenges for me through this process was that I was in a constant state of denial because I couldn't wrap my mind around the fact that this person, who presented herself as a godly person, that presented herself as a good woman, a good mother, someone that's faithful, someone that's dedicated, someone that's kind, someone that presented herself as being considerate, and thoughtful, was this cold and callous. Because the image that I had of her did not match the actions I was being shown, I would constantly reject what I was being shown. Later, I learned that I was rejecting the voice of God, because when we receive an intuition hit or are given a discernment concerning something, that's the spiritual realm, God speaking to us, or our angels warning us of things that are going on around us that we can't see or don't know about.

Part of my healing journey was healing of my intuition and discernment from continually disregarding the voice of God, which I had to repent for. One lesson I would share with you, to allow you to know if the thought that you're receiving is your own or you're receiving it from the spiritual realm, is this: would you normally think that your spouse is cheating of your own thought process? If you wouldn't, then it's probably coming from the spiritual realm, which has a warning. If the thought process is outside of your normal process, that's how I know if it's my thoughts or it's thoughts from the spiritual realm. I would have never thought that my ex-partner would have been unfaithful, lied, cheated, stole, been involved with spell work, and conducted smear campaigns to try to hinder my business and my job. But now that I've seen it, felt it and lived it, I know that she's able to do everything that I thought she would never do. And I'm grateful for the lesson because, again, any person who comes into our life to teach us lessons.

Lesson one that I needed to learn was to love myself. Part of loving yourself is considering yourself in every single activity and everything that you do. If you're giving to others and it's hurting you, then that's not self-love. Self-love requires that you at least consider how, of course, something will harm or affect someone else but also how it will affect you. There's a Biblical verse that says, "Love your neighbor as you love yourself," but throughout that process, I forgot about myself. My only focus was loving, helping, and taking care of others.

The second lesson I needed to learn was how to say no. "No" is a complete answer, a complete thought. No does not need an explanation. No is setting and healthy boundary, which is needed if you are a person that is aspiring to live a healthy, balanced life. You have to learn to say no.

Lesson 3 was people-pleasing. I had to learn to stop being a people-pleaser. The first time that I heard that statement said to me that I was a people-pleaser was from my attorney, Jeff D. I was involved with a case where someone was trying to present a lawsuit against me and a business partner on a house flip that we had done. At this particular meeting, my attorney, Jeff, told to me that this is why I was in this lawsuit; because I was a people-pleaser, because I was getting this person everything that they wanted; and when I stopped, it's when they got angry with me and wanted to find a way of getting back at me. The people-pleasing part of my life was a part, I believe, that was incubated within me from my youth. Because I come from a line of pastors—my grandfather and my father were both pastors. I saw them serve, I saw them give, I saw them give up themselves, go above and beyond, and often I would use that as an excuse as to why I did the same. But then, one day, I looked around at my siblings and I discovered that none of them had the same issue. So, at that point, I stopped using that as an excuse and I started looking at that as something again, that I had to address. I could not deny it.

Writing was very pivotal for me throughout this healing process.

Some people might call it journaling, I just call it writing because often I would get a notebook and feel inspired to write about the events that were taking place around my life. Mainly because I was all alone; and because I was alone, there were times when I got tired of just talking to myself, LOL. Because even though I'm a loner naturally, when you've been around people, family, and sons, you go through a process where you miss them. This is part of the reality of a long-term relationship breaking up; it often splinters in one direction or the other. It generally isn't an even split, and usually, according to studies, men are gently left alone, whether they were faithful in the relationship and committed or not. One of the lessons that I learned through the healing process in writing was that I would stay in my suffering longer than I was supposed to because I kept denying the events that were taking place. There's a quote I read that stands out in this moment, and that quote is, *"Pain is inevitable, but suffering is optional."*

So, what that means in layman's terms is that we could have a painful experience take place within our lives, and it could be something as simple as hitting your hand with a hammer or putting your hand in hot water. Hitting your hand once is pain, but continually hitting it is suffering; the same thing with the water example: if hot water hits your skin, it's pain, but suffering represents that you stick your hand in boiling hot water for extended periods of time. When you stay in these unhealthy, damaging, toxic, harmful relationships for extended periods of time, it's suffering.

The good news is you will start feeling relief and a sense of peace and joy when you can remove yourself from these unhealthy relationships. It's when you can remove yourself from that energy and get to a place of peace, of healing, of self-discovery, and of joy that you can actually start remembering "Who You Are" and living your life based on your own terms. This start isn't based upon your age, race, gender, or education; it's based on your desire for change, and a hope for a brighter future, and longing for love that's not abusive, but love that's true, honest, pure, without boundaries, and full of peace.

A personal story of denial comes to mind as I write this chapter. I had a family friend who is getting up in age and has a spouse that has been sick for a while. Whenever I would talk to her about the possibilities of his passing, she would brush the conversation off; she wasn't open to having this conversation. I can understand why she's denying the conversation, because of all of the years and time that they had been with each other, and there's probably a part of her mind that can't imagine him not being here. So, denial is a form of self-protection in this particular example or story.

But it's also what I found from personal experience; it makes something that's natural, and that's innate for everyone to happen in their life more difficult because of not accepting the fact that this person will pass at some point. Just because we deny something or don't accept it does not mean that it's not going to happen anyway. But when we can face this fact—when we can start accepting the fact that there are things outside of our control that are going to happen — we can feel more confident in handling them. Always remember that denial is a defense mechanism that we innately have within ourselves, but it also can turn a painful situation into a suffering situation.

Imagine, if you will, with me that there are two friends, one named Tina and one named Kim, and over a period of time, there was a rift of some sort in the relationship. Tina came to Kim to talk to her about it, but Kim denied the situation. She didn't see that it was a problem and she felt that it was all in Tina's head; she felt like that everything was okay and told Tina to just leave it alone—everything is okay. So, over a period of time, nothing was resolved, and because of differences in interests and because of differences and goals, they ended up going their separate ways.

Now, imagine that that is your relationship, and you have come, pleaded, and tried to compel your companion to see what you are saying concerning the relationship. But they, like Kim, refuse to hear, and over time, it was the collapse of the relationship. Denial doesn't mean that the event we are denying won't happen; it just means that, because we didn't face the issue, it's still going to happen, but when it does, you won't be ready because of being stuck in the energy of denial. Denial is deception to yourself—not wanting to face the inevitable.

If you are reading this book or listening, you, like myself, may have denied what your partner or spouse has done or is doing, and it was done from a place of not believing that they could do these things. So, the first stage that you will have that naturally evolves into as you heal will be the stage of denial.

> "Denial can be a powerful defense mechanism but it can also be a trap."

> "Denial is a refusal to believe the truth even though it is staring you in your face."

> "Denial is a luxury you can't afford when facing reality."

Affirmation:

say this five times with me, **"I am open, receptive, and excited to receive revelation that may be hard to receive initially but that I know is for my benefit."**

Take time right now to do some writing on denial.

Question number one: What is something that you denied concerning your relationship that you see now clearly?

Question number two: Freely write about the denial process for you. Write as much as you can on this topic and process. This is an important part of your healing because, as you start accepting what you are seeing, it will allow you not to get hurt so often.

Spend quality time daily journaling.

Hit this link to gain access to an exclusive private healing community: http://www.skool.com/healing-hearts-community-3442

Go follow me on youtube: https://www.youtube.com/channel/UCBHsTrBoLNDIzbEh8oTtVeg

The link to all of my social media can be found on youtube.

5. ANGER

nger is a strong emotional response characterized by feelings of frustration, irritation, and hostility. It is also triggered by perceived threats, and injustices, and frustrations. Anger is a natural emotion that all of us have felt at some point in our lives. When you glance at the definition of feeling frustrated, irritated, or hostility that is triggered by a threat or injustice, many of us have felt that irritation or pain of Injustice. There is a part of us that desires justice, that things be made balanced or fair. When you are in your healing journey, part of it that's an invisible trap is allowing yourself to get blinded by the rage of what was done to you. This part of the healing journey is the most critical part and most crucial part. This is the part where many will get stuck along the healing journey and not be able to move from it, because it takes all of our attention from ourselves, and the focus is on someone or something else.

We need to go back over the steps that were taken to get to this point: first, you were in shock, and then you moved on to denial. Once you're in denial and see how senseless the acts were that caused all of this pain and all of the injustice that were a direct result or consequence of those actions from someone else, this is when anger sets in. When anger sets in, you will want someone to pay for what they have done. The thing that I would like to stress to you about this particular stage is that anger is a normal emotion. We are taught, biblically, to "be angry but sin not," so even from a Biblical or religious perspective, anger is mentioned as a normal emotion. When you go through the process of someone betraying you, doing deceptive things behind your back, stealing from you, dealing in dark magic, putting things in your food to control you, lying—when you come to the revelation of that after you move from denial—you will definitely go through a stage of anger, because it's senseless, and because you will be hurt. And the hurt that you feel, you will feel in your body, in your heart, for the loss.

When you discover that the person that you loved and that said they loved you that they never knew how to love, and that you never actually knew them, and that it was all an act, and it was all deception, and that they didn't really care about you and how the things that they did would affect you, and you know this by their actions, regardless of what they said—their actions showed that they did not care. The thing about anger is that it is not always in the energy of full aggression; it can be passive. But, regardless, it is the trap that many that are on this journey get entangled in. It's not until you can move past all of the anger.

Some of the things that I did that helped me get past all of the anger were a prayer for many who know me and for those who don't, my story is a story of being a third-generation pastor's son, so I learned at a very young age about the importance of prayer. I was raised in a very Pentecostal-style church, so we believed in praying with emotion fervent tears. Also meditation on my heart; I learned some heart-centered meditations which allowed me to release many things. The benefit of prayer for me was that it was me sending a petition or request to God, to the universe, or to whatever terminology you use. The benefit of meditation was it allowed me to sit in that prayer place in silence, open to receive. Part of the openness of receiving is even your hands, as you sit your palm should be up, your heart should be open, and you should be in anticipation and expectation of a direction (if you join our private community, all of the techniques are taught in detail.)

One of the keys, that is very important, was the heart-centered meditations, because on your healing journey, you will feel as if you were more healed than you are throughout this process. In theory, you will be healing, but the emotional part of our healing is one of the most critical parts of the healing process. This process deals with our heart, so there has to be a lot of time spent on your heart, on opening your heart, and on not hardening your heart. Understand that the difficulty that you went through was a test of your heart, to see if you would still be open.

I started this chapter by saying many get stuck in this particular part of the healing journey because it feels really good; it feels justified. It feels like what you're supposed to do is to get at someone, to hate someone, to alienate everybody, to feel like all men are bad, or all women are bad, or all people are bad, which, in theory, has to be wrong and not true. It's just that the person you discovered was a person sent to test you, to test your heart. A revelation I received personally was that if I allowed those that had inflicted the mistreatment upon me to still dwell in my heart through all of my hatred, anger, bitterness, and resentment, then I would eventually become a disciple of theirs. I would go out, hurt other people, disrespect other people, and harm other people based upon my heart not being healed but broken and shattered.

Some of the things that helped me through the process of healing, and especially my heart, was journaling. I learned to write daily, expressing what I was feeling, why I was feeling what I was feeling, and how unjust I felt things were. Why did I have to go to these things? I would ask these type of questions because I was still unsure as to why all of these events took place when I felt like I was a good person and bad things shouldn't happen to a good person whose only intent was to do good to others.

So, I started journaling. I got involved with a healing group out of New Mexico. I blocked all of my social medias from the only one that was involved with me and my ex, that took her side, and any close associates that were involved. I started working out five times a week (now it's up to six times a week), eating cleaner and healthier. I cut out most alcohol I just focused on myself. I started filling my mind with good e-books, watching videos with laughter or that were comic in nature. I started to rebuild myself, brick by brick.

It was through this process of soft focus that I decided that I would not lend my energy to someone who clearly didn't give an ounce of thought about me and who didn't deserve my energy. And if I was angry towards them, constantly talking about them, thinking about them, and feeling angry with them, I was giving them my energy—because where attention goes, energy flows. So, at this point in life, this is where I decided and refused to invest where there wasn't a mutual exchange of benefits.

At some point as you rebuild yourself, you won't have a more concentrated focus on your growth and your boundaries. Because as you grow, different revelation will be revealed to you about yourself. For me, one thing I needed to learn was to be obedient to my internal voice, my intuition, my discernment, how to set healthy boundaries, how to say no, and most importantly, to have total and complete love for myself. When I refer to having love for yourself, I'm not saying love for yourself in a narcissistic way; I'm talking about now considering yourself when in the past, you didn't. I'm talking about no longer taking the back seat in life and being considerate of others more than you are of yourself—to take care of yourself physically, mentally, emotionally, and spiritually.

At this point, I want you to give yourself a little contract in your journal. I want you to write between you and those individuals that you are going to release today. Starting today, you are releasing these individuals out of your life because they no longer have any power, any strength, any thought, any dominion. You have no more care concerning them and the things that they're doing with their lives, because you are in the process of creating a new, exciting life.

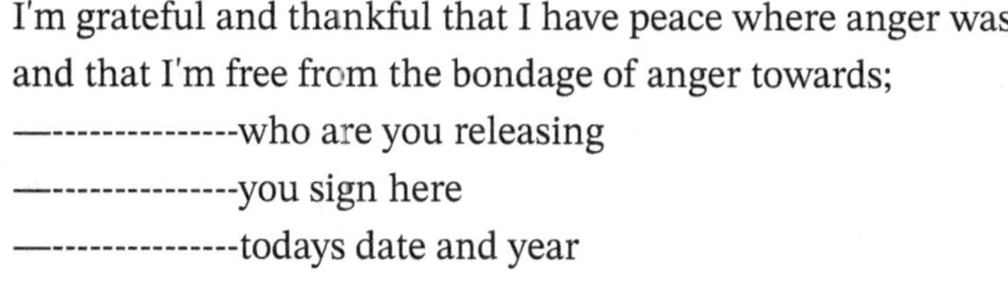

I'm grateful and thankful that I have peace where anger was
and that I'm free from the bondage of anger towards;
————————who are you releasing
————————you sign here
————————todays date and year

Another technique that I'll share is that read that statement, record it, recite it, and play it while you're getting ready in the morning, while you're ready to go to sleep at night, or while you're just driving in your vehicle, because you want to start getting into the energy, start feeling it, and knowing for a fact that it's true. You will know when it's true that you have released this individual when you are no longer triggered by them, and you are in the energy of not caring at all. This is an important step in regaining your power back.

One of my personal motivations doing my healing was that I didn't want to be the typical angry guy, and the only way that I could move past the anger was by healing. When we heal, that spirit of anger can't stay concerning that particular challenge. Now, it might be a part of another challenge, but gaining victory over my past relationship was priority number one. The catastrophic results of not doing it would be that I would have walked around like a ticking time bomb, ready to explode in an instant, always triggered, unknowingly being controlled by someone. The worst part would have been going out, meeting another unexpected woman, mistreating her, cheating on her, and just spreading more of the toxic energy in the world. I knew I didn't want to do that to others like what was done to me, especially because of how intense the pain was. And again, I did not want to become a disciple of destruction, which represents people that never consider healing after relationships trauma. Because they were hurt and taken advantage of, they go out, find another, and continue to duplicate the same thing over and over, not realizing that there is a spiritual price to pay for intensely hurting other people.

Just because you were hurt, that doesn't give you the right to go out and hurt other people. There is another option: you can decide to heal. That's going to require you to reevaluate yourself. You will do an introspection, a deep dive on where all of your anger originated. During my deep dive, I'm not sure why I was quick to anger even as a child. Up until early teen, I would have major blowouts and fits of anger. Some of it was, when I look back, because I was quiet and didn't like expressing my thoughts. I would keep things bottled up inside of me until one day it would explode like a bomb going off. I would explode, and the only person that could control me was my dad, in those times. I had a healthy fear and respect for him, and when I would hear his voice, it would stop me in my tracks.

As I started journaling and writing about my life, I would often reflect on the past and the fact that my life was simple and easy, and I didn't have a justifiable reason for anger. I had loving parents. I grew up in a Godly household where we would sit at the dinner table every night, where my our father would make us communicate and talk, and made sure that we were seen and heard, as well as our mom. But for whatever reason, anger was something that I remember being an issue for me. It was through journaling that I realized that my anger was generally directed towards injustice that I saw concerning others, more so than something that was done directly to me.

The simple revelation that anger represented that I was being controlled by some other person or some other circumstance. Not being willing to allow that to happen, but refusing to allow it to happen—because if everything that they say, everything that they do ticks you off, makes you mad, has you in your feelings, has you on some emotional rant, then they are controlling you. It's like you're a puppet on your string, and they are living rent-free in your mind, in your body, and in your emotions. I say, no way, Jose—that's no bueno. It's time to stand up; it's time to, you know, be angry that you were used, that you were taking advantage of, but also to get angry enough to stand up for yourself and look at how you can start changing your life for the better.

So then, the next step would be learning to control yourself, to be a person of temperance, to be at peace. Meditation silencing my mind gave me victory over those things, along with prayer. The thing with meditation is that it allowed me to start gaining back control of my mind. When you do a deep dive on meditation, they consider meditation to be equivalent to working out on our bodies, as meditation is to our minds.

Poem; *"He who angers you conquers you."*

— ELIZABETH KENNY

Poem; *Speak when you are angry, you will make the best speech you will ever regret.*

— AMBROSE BIERCE

Poem; *To be angry is to be human, to control anger is to be wise.*

This is the story of the broken bridge. There were two villages connected by a beautiful bridge. One day, a quarrel between villagers led to its destruction. Realizing their mistake, they rebuilt it stronger than before, learning that anger destroys but understanding rebuilds. This quote applies in our lives: "If you stay in the energy of anger and resentment, you will keep yourself in a destructive pattern. For when you are understanding and forgiving, you can rebuild."

In order to rebuild from what happened in that relationship, you have to forgive and move on from it. The rebuilding is of yourself, where you will no longer be in the energy and control of others.

Affirmation;

"I'm grateful, thankful, and excited that I have taken my

power back, that I gave freely to others who didn't appreciate it." Say this five times

The echoing cave

There was a young traveler who entered a cave and shouted in anger, only to be met with a fierce echo that frightened him. Then, realizing his own voice was his enemy, he learned to speak softly, and the echo softened too. Anger begets anger; speak gently, and peace will answer.

In the midst of being hurt by your partner, you will get angry, and you will lash out, cuss, and maybe even scream. But at some point, as you embark on this journey, the hurt and pain has lessons, and you will be able to speak in a softer manner, mainly because you would have grown over time as you have gone through your process.

My Hope, prayer, and desire for you is that you don't allow the stage of anger to start taking a root in your life after you find out about the betrayals. What I found, through my own personal experience, is that it was like falling in quicksand: the more I fought and was resentful and bitter, the more joy and happiness the person who caused the pain had. They were glad I was in pain because this gave them a sense of being important or that they had some value in my life, even though it was through a negative emotion.

You suck all the life out of them by being willing to heal, to be alone, to pray, to meditate, to journal, to focus on yourself, and to release them from all that they have done. To the point that you realize how much of a benefit this whole event has been to you in your life and how it was time for you to move on, grow, and become, because you probably would have already outgrown this person anyway. The breakup was just the confirmation from the 3D reality that you are no longer aligned.

If, through the process of reading this book, you feel as though you want to be part of our healing community as a member, reach out to the author directly on social media. He has links on all of his pages; the easiest page that you can reach to and get all of them is the YouTube page:

https://www.youtube.com/channel/UCBHsTrBoLNDIzbEh8o TtVeg

Hit this link to join our exclusive healing community:

http://www.skool.com/healing-hearts-community-3442

6. BARGAINING

*B*argaining. By the time you got to the bargaining stage, you would have denied that the betrayal had happened. You would have also been in a stage of unbelief or shock. You would have, after that, started to receive insight that would have moved you into anger, and the anger would be as a result of how senseless the acts were and feeling the pain of injustice.

So by time you start getting into actually working on your healing through prayers and meditation, you will, at some point throughout your prayers, get to a point of crying out to God, to the Most High, to the universe, and asking for help and asking for understanding. Through that, what I found that I ended up doing was I started moving into the bargaining stage, where I was asking God for certain things like, "Can you take this pain away from me? If you take this pain away from me, I will acknowledge you before I get in another relationship. If you take this pain from my heart, give me relief, please; I will do what you want me to do. Allow my heart to be restored, new and whole again."

I would seek God in fervent prayer, praying out my heart with tears many days because the pain in my heart—the heartbreak—was too much to handle at times. On top of all of that, I was alone most of the time. I only had my parents that I could rely on, but at this time, my dad had gone through a stroke, and I didn't want to add any more weight to my mom than what she was already going through. So what I would do is I would go over on Saturdays, and I would have prayer with them, and partially the prayer was for me, but the prayer was also for them and the things that they were going through.

This part of being alone was directly attributed to the smear campaigns that had been promoted by my now ex-wife and her mother, different family members of mine, and different people who were close to me that knew me for many years. They took great delight in speaking evil about me, saying certain things and accusing me of things that I had never done, and defending the person who was the cause of the breakup and the destruction of the relationship, which was very hurtful. But it was also still a part of the process of going through the stages of no longer denying who these people actually were, but accepting it and getting past the anger and getting to a place of forgiveness.

The one main thing that I did wrong was I tried to love a person or someone that said that they wanted love, that they wanted a family, that they wanted a home, that wanted a loving relationship. These are all of the things that she said she wanted, but evidently, that wasn't true. My only agenda and thought while I was married was to provide for and take care of my family and also get myself to the point where I had things set up financially for my kids, and eventually, my grandkids. So I was trying at this stage to negotiate with God and ask for relief. I needed to feel whole again because I was completely broken, again okay, and broke again.

My negotiations in bargaining were from a place of pain. As was your pain, if you are like me, you made promises to God of things that you would do when you get better or out of this painful challenge. At this time, you may start getting revelations of what your calling or purpose on this Earth is. This is where it was revealed to me that I needed to go through these events, and through it, I was going to help other people all over the world learn to heal themselves with my story and how I was able to go from burnt down into ash to the reborn phoenix rising from the ash.

It's important in the bargaining that you find your purpose, which represents what you are going to be used for to help others. As you find that, it will be a source to help you move towards your healing because you know there is a powerful destiny that's connected to your life, which is connected to other people. But you know you have to accomplish or do bargaining which is kind of a funny stage; I'm not saying funny like laughter; I'm saying funny like different. It's where we are in dire straits, we are in trouble, and we are calling out to God and asking for help, but in the process of all of this, you are trying to sell the spiritual realm or God on your proposition.

So then, when your purpose is highlighted, it will help to smooth out the whole process because now that you have an idea of why that event was in your life, what the purpose behind it was, and what you are supposed to do with everything that you have learned, then you can approach the Creator, the universe, the Most High, from a place of power. Because the storm, the breakup, the divorce, the betrayal, many times happens to get you to see what else you can do with your life.

So you can bargain with the fact that it's God's will that you do these things. Over a period of time, through much prayer, meditation, journaling, and joining into groups and communities for healing, you will see that it's a lot easier because you will have others who will have success stories. You will hear how others have had difficulties, and you will not feel alone. You will be a part of a group that is all going in similar directions.

According to a study by Dominican University:

1. When you do a thing with a group, you will have a higher success rate than doing it alone;
2. When you write down your goals and are specific with dates, you have a higher success rate;

3. Commit to act on the goals that you have, and you need to have regular updates to the group, which will guarantee your success because of the accountability of others.

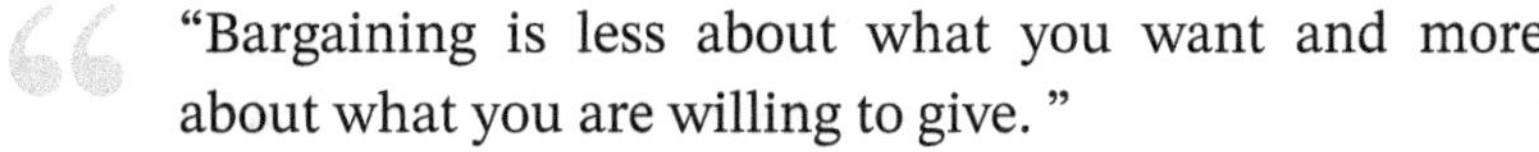

"Bargaining is less about what you want and more about what you are willing to give. "

— UNKNOWN AUTHOR

"In grief, we negotiate with our emotions, trying to find peace amidst the pain."

A part of the bargaining stage that needs to be discussed is the stage that I was in many times. It would happen in prayer that I would go through a process of saying my spiritual resume to God, telling God all the things that I had done good for people—that I was faithful, that my heart was pure, that I had only good intentions in my heart, and that I was providing. I was dependable, and I was doing all that I knew to do. I was helping other people, supporting people, and I didn't understand why this was happening to me. Because at this point, my eyes were not open, like yours probably weren't either, to see the good or the seed of equal benefit.

Now, all you see is pain, loss, and discouragement in the sense that you just wasted all of the time; all of those years were for nothing. But over time, you will see that this is far from the truth. Often, we associate a bargain with getting a good deal on something we buy, at some place that we have gone, or at some event. While you are negotiating, your point is part of wanting a restoration of the balance that is lacking right now.

The point I would like to stress to you is that these stages aren't linear. You will maneuver from stage to Stage throughout your healing process. It's when or if you don't desire to heal is when you will get stuck in a perpetual stage of anger, as an example. So grow in Grace and in a knowledge of the Most High.

7. DEPRESSION

It is often said that anxiety is when we are worried about the future and that depression is when we are worried about the past. Depression is inevitable as you go through the stages of grief; it's inevitable because, by the time you get past being in a state of shock to denial that the events have had taken place, to win you move past denial and start grasping what has happened, and that it was such a senseless act of selflessness and betrayal that caused so much unnecessary hurt and pain—that's when, even though acceptance is the final stage, I felt like, personally, the beginning and genesis of acceptance started in the process of the anger stage. Because when we are in the anger stage, that's when we are actually starting to grasp and to accept the things that have happened, and because of the injustice, that's where, again, the anger is initiated.

Depression was a difficult stage for me; one reason was because I was unaware of what was happening or going on in my life. I was still functioning, getting up every day, going to work, motivating others, doing all of the things in the past that I had done. The difference was that I would have days of feeling deeply low and not motivated, days of severe discouragement.

I was discouraged with God, and when I think back on it, my

discouragement with God was because I got caught in the trap of comparing my life to others around me. There's a quote that says that comparison is the thief of joy. That statement is very true because when we start comparing our lives and the things that are going on in our lives with others, and we don't know what the path of their lives is, it will discourage you, because it will make you think that they have it easier than you.

The thing that was so ironic about this stage was different negative events that would happen that normally I could handle easily; when I was in the stage of depression, I noticed later on, after getting out of it, that it was harder for me to get past small events or negative events that happened throughout a day when I was in the stage of depression.

When you are looking at other people's lives and wondering why good things aren't happening for you—and you know you're a good person, you go to church, you love people, you give to those that are less fortunate, you are kind, you study the Bible or your holy books, you learn—of course, there's always room that you can do more. But you are experiencing just hardship after hardship; it was as if no relief was in sight.

On top of that, I felt alone. Even though I was in a marriage, I didn't feel support from the person who verbally would tell me that I could count on them, that they were my support, and that they had my back. Also, I had someone who had falsely accused a business partner and myself of doing inappropriate things in a business deal. Because of all of the weight I felt in my life, there were days that I just felt like, "Why can't I catch a break? When will I get the blessings that the minister is always talking about?"

It was a stage of my life that I lost belief—my belief in God or a higher power—and it was based upon knowing that I had done the right thing for almost 30 years. Why was I still struggling when things turned around? It wasn't until one day that my mom, who, to those that know her, they know her to be a powerful spiritual individual with a prophetic gift, it was either revealed to her that I was in a state of depression and that the events going on were part of a process of me getting a story, but also I needed to learn these lessons. In that, the lessons and the wisdom from the lessons were going to be a blessing to help heal and teach people to heal themselves all over the world.

This was the prophetic message that was given to me through my mother in the year of 2017, which predated the events that took place by almost 2023. I was never a person through the process of depression that felt like I ever wanted to take my life; I felt like I just needed a break or relief from all the events and all the pressure. Before I found out about the infidelity of my ex, the financial portrayals, all the lies and manipulation, and how she was not actually with me—yes, she was physically in the same house, but her heart was for everyone else and everything else—which now as I'm writing this, my spirit could have started grieving even before I found out in this 3D reality. Our spiritual part, or subconscious mind, knows the things that we are not aware of.

In closing, this point of depression was as a result of events in my life. Regardless of whether I prayed or not, I would get relief for a week or so, but there would be a day that a load of bad things would happen, and I couldn't handle it, which wasn't like me. I would classify myself then as a functional depressed person. When I would hear songs, I would cry; I would be driving somewhere alone and just start crying.

I understand now the quote that says, "When you are happy, you enjoy the music, but when you are sad, you understand the lyrics." It's by Frank Ocean. The lyrics are very meaningful when you are in a sad state; it's as if they come to life. One of the things that was unknown to me, which you may be able to relate to, is that because I wasn't by nature a depressed person, I didn't categorize myself, based on the descriptions out there, as someone who was in the state of depression or stage of depression. I would place it in the category of being discouraged spiritually based on my religious background. Another point is many people in your life, if you are considered the strong person the person—that's the encourager, the motivator, the uplifter, the one that is successful—many people around you won't necessarily consider that you're in a difficult time. They're so conditioned and used to seeing you on top and strong that, even if you confided in them and say something, I found that many people would joke off things and assume you're okay, and you know, make it, make a joke out of it and brush it off. That's the advice that you will hear many times, and if you are that person in that time frame, they will add insult to injury.

The ironic thing that was also going on at this time was that I had two clients that I met and I was working for, submitting bids, setting up their projects, getting things ordered, and things along that line. Because at this stage, I was still building a construction company/real estate development company. I had built a nice following on social media, so I would get calls often and invitations to do joint ventures.

The first project that I'm telling you about was a young Brazilian woman that I met who was from North Jersey, that was living in New Jersey because her mom had passed away, and she was staying in Jersey to be close to the remainder of her family that she had left. When we initially met for the first meeting, she was very motivated, very excited, very on top of things, very disciplined, concerning the project. This young woman, who I'll call Maritza, was involved in the project. She was able to be reached by phone, text, email, etc., for whatever was needed. Once the project started, it was as if she became Casper the Friendly Ghost—she never answered the phone, no return calls, no emails—which caused me to get a little delusion with the project to the point where I was thinking about just quitting the project and walking away from it.

As fate would have it, I had the number of her business partner, Mario. What I would get in contact with him? He would relay the message to Maritza, and a few days later, I will hear from her. Sometime later, I found out that she wasn't in the USA; but that she had gone to Brazil to reconnect with people that she had known in the past and she missed.

One day, as all these events were happening, she came back to New Jersey and we set up an appointment to meet that particular day, so we could go over the project again. As we were walking through the project and having a casual conversation, as we walked through the house, she started crying—not in a hysterical way, but in an uncontrollable way, almost as if she didn't want to, but she couldn't hold it in.

So I asked her, "Do you mind me asking what is wrong? Are you okay? How can I help you?" By me asking these questions and because we had built a professional friendship at that point, she began to tell me of all of the things that had been going on, how that she had lost her mom, who she was really close to, and that she no longer was with her boyfriend of 10 years, how she doesn't get out of bed for days at a time, she can't eat, and she's not motivated anymore about making money or this house. I just listened to her without in interjecting, but I knew as she was talking what it was—she was in a state of depression. Because of the two people that were most important in her life, she had lost them both in a short period of time, and the losses were too close. She had invested so much of her heart into them that she felt like giving up, and that she had no value and that nothing mattered to her anymore. I told her about my experiences and what I had been through, and also the techniques I found that worked for me. I invited her to join my daily a.m. meditation prayer session I was having. I also shared some info about Dr. Joe Dispenza with her and promised to her that I would help her through this if she wanted my help.

Then, two weeks after this episode, I was referred to a building project in Atlantic City, New Jersey, by one of my family members. My family member worked with this individual, so I ended up going over to the customer's house. And as I did, again, like the last event, I had just finished walking through the job and was sitting at the client's table. As we were having small talk, she started getting teary-eye and crying. Again, I asked, "Are you okay? Do you want to talk about it? How can I help?" So I listened as the client told me the story of how she had lost her husband of almost 30 years recently and that she was having difficulties with dealing with it.

She told me the story of him telling her, "Baby, I'm going to run down to the store and get something." He put on his helmet, got on his motorcycle, and the next thing she knew was that she was getting a call from the police department to come and identify him. Evidently, he had a motorcycle accident and was deceased on the scene; someone had hit him. And of course, because I had just spoken to Maritza two weeks ago and had also had my own experiences, I knew she was dealing with depression. The one thing that kind of kept her afloat was she had several sons who were high school age, and she needed to keep it together for them.

So again, I offered my help as far as, you know, the a.m. prayer/meditation, and I introduced her to Dr. Joe's teachings on meditation and the mind. But also, it was glaringly aware that this was an answer to a prayer I was seeking: what was the direction that my life was supposed to go in? What is my purpose that I need to bring to humanity? This is where my personal clarity started. I knew somehow I was supposed to help people who were in some difficulty get relief.

Depression isn't a one-size-fits-all; it's a variation of people from different backgrounds, ages, and the economic backgrounds that are affected by depression. The commonality is that the person is at a low state vibrationally. To give you an example, look at how many describe how they are feeling: sad, discouraged, defeated, lost, hopeless, downtrodden, disillusioned, feeling there is no hope, all is lost, and giving up. Again, I'm going to reiterate a quote that I started this with. It said that anxiety is when we are worried about our future, and depression is when we are focused on the past. It may be a tough challenge, but now is the time to focus on the endless possibilities that are available to you through your suffering. For some, there will be a revelation that's brought to life that will help you see what is your purpose and calling, and how you can help others to come out of their difficulties like you did.

As I ponder on this topic of depression, I remember a story that happened when I was about 12 years old. I came home from school and heard my mom. I could hear her crying in her room. I asked one of my sisters what was wrong, what happened, why was Mom crying? And my sister told me that Mom was crying because the woman she worked for, Mrs. bini's son, had passed away. He had a go-kart accident and passed away, and after he passed away, because of the sadness of losing her son, who was about 12 years old, she end up going into a tailspin and into depression, and she ended up taking her own life. So my first experience with the topic of depression and suicide was when I heard about Mrs. Bini. How it made me feel as a 12-year-old at that time was I couldn't understand it. I couldn't relate to it; I couldn't relate to anything being that drastic or powerful to make you want to take your own life.

Partially because of my religious background, it didn't make any sense to me why someone would take their own life, why they would commit suicide. Again, this was from the mind of a 12-year-old. I thought that someone would have to be weak to do something like that, partially because I just did not understand it. You know, I don't feel that way now. I understand that there are some that don't have a source where they can release a lot of the pressures of life. And because of it, and because of how low their energy is in the vibrational match of where they are, they feel like there's no other alternative for them to do than that.

But the thing that I wanted to stress with this chapter, and to let people know, is that there are options. There are other options that you can take, whether it's the depression from a failed relationship, the passing of a loved one, or the loss of a substantial amount of financial resources. These things will pass. There will be new people that you meet, there will be other business deals that you can acquire, and your loved ones who passed are still with you. If you have taken the time to build those memories and you still talk about them and think about them, they're still with you.

This is why, from a biblical mindset, we are commanded to cast our cares upon the Almighty because He cares for us. When we don't cast off our worries, pains, gripes, or discouragements, they will multiply, they will grow, and eventually, they will explode. This will be because of denying the situation instead of facing it. Denial does not mean that the result still won't come to pass; it means that we won't be ready when it does come to pass because we are not accepting it.

> "The pain that you feel today is the strength that you will feel tomorrow."
>
> — UNKNOWN AUTHOR

> "When you come out of the storm, you won't be the same person that entered it."
>
> — UNKNOWN AUTHOR

> "Difficult roads often lead to beautiful destinations."
>
> — ZIG ZIGLAR

An important key that I learned in this stage of depression is that it is important that we monitor where we are when it comes to comparing ourselves to our previous partner or past spouse. If you are watching their social media and seeing all of their supposed "wins," it will make you feel defeated, especially if you were the one who fought for the relationship, and you sacrificed, and tried everything you could to make it work, especially if you are seeing them online with a new person that they are presenting as if they are so much better than you—that's all an act. This is why I suggest to those I have coached that you eliminate everything concerning that past relationship, close it out, and throw it out. Give it away; get it out of your energy, out of your life, and out of your thoughts as much as possible.

As I'm writing this chapter, the story—the real-life story—of a gentleman named Kevin Hines comes to mind. At age 19, Kevin was struggling with severe mental issues, including bipolar disorder and depression. On Saturday, the 25th of 2000, he made the decision to jump from the Golden Gate Bridge in California. Immediately after jumping, Kevin experienced moments of regret and realized he wanted to live. Fortunately, he survived the fall, which is remarkable given that many who jump from that particular bridge don't make it. Kevin was rescued by the Coast Guard and received medical attention for his injuries. He mentioned that when he hit the water, he could feel certain bones in his spine were broken, and he couldn't move.

After his recovery, Kevin became an advocate for the kids for mental health awareness and suicide prevention. One of the things that stood out to me as I read his story was that, when he was home, before he left to go to the Golden Gate Bridge, he wrote letters to his parents and to his sibling. When he left, he talked about being on a bus, crying in the back of the bus, and he said that what he desired most in that moment was that someone would actually see him, that they would actually see him for who he was. So when he arrived, got off the bus, and struggled to make the decision of what he was going to do, he was saying within his mind, "Please, somebody talk me out of this, somebody see me, somebody help me." At one point, there was a couple that came up to him and they asked him, "Do you mind taking a picture for us?" He said after he took the picture for this couple, his decision was final, and that's when he jumped.

But again, the good news is that Kevin survived and that he's an advocate for mental health awareness and for depression. Just know that you are not the only one; there are others who are in difficult and challenging times. This is part of one of the reasons why I provide a community for those who are coming out of relationship trauma. Hit the link to join our community: https://www.skool.com/signup?ref=8c07290a7de0437cabe93bb46041d266

To gain access to our exclusive private healing community
Hit the link: www.skool.com/healing-hearts-community-3442

8. ACCEPTANCE

Acceptance is the first part to healing. As a child growing up, I can remember hearing a story of how my parents met each other. They met as teenagers, ended up getting married very young, and because of that, the jobs that they generally had were office cleanings, factory work, and things along those lines. But as my dad got older, in his 40s, I remember very clearly that he started going to college based upon an associate he met who encouraged him to go. When he ended up graduating, which took quite a lot longer than it would if he was just a regular full-time student instead of a husband, father, and student, he ended up getting a degree in something involving substance abuse counseling.

As he moved into that profession, as a teenager sitting at our dinner table at night, he would talk about the different events that had taken place in his work and the different clients that he was working with and he dealt with. He would teach lessons to my siblings and myself about things that we should be careful of and watch for as we navigate this thing called life.

I talk about acceptance because even though my dad hadn't been to school approximately 30 years at that point, he didn't allow his present situation to define his future. This is the same thing that I'm suggesting for you as you're reading and/or listening to this book:

that you are not going to allow the events that have transpired in your past to dictate your future events, but that you're going to come to a place of acceptance—not of the condition that you're in, but acceptance of possibility that this relationship that you have been in for maybe several decades or years has run its course, and that the person that you thought loved you, based upon their behavior, you might need to accept that they never actually loved you.

You might need to accept that they never really cared but that they were actually using you. You might need to accept that you're going to have to be on your own again. You might need to accept that you don't have all of the details of your next steps, but you just believe that somehow all of these things are working together for a much better benefit and purpose for your life. You have to accept that things happening in our lives are happening for our benefit. Many times, it is challenging to see the positive when we are initially in the situation, but over a period of time, as we go through, as we sit back, as we heal, as we acknowledge the Creator, as we ask, and as we meditate, the revelation of why we went through what we went through and what were we supposed to learn through it, will be magnified and will be illuminated to us.

When I shared with you the example of my parents, there were certain things that they had to accept. Because of getting married as teenagers, they had to accept the jobs they had at that time. They had to accept, when they initially got married, that they lived with their in-laws until they could make enough money to buy their first home. Sometimes, acceptance is a source of motivation because either we can sit back, complain, gripe, moan, and blame, or we can get up and believe that we can change our situations, that our lives have purpose, and that we have a clear destiny and reason for our existence. You have it within you to figure it out if you really desire it. Whatever you desire, when you pray, ask, believing, knowing that it is done without doubting, and you shall have what you are saying.

Through my dad's new job, one of the things that really stuck with me was the Prayer of Serenity that he taught us, which he mentioned numerous times. The part that comes to mind as most appropriate for this chapter of the book is learning to accept the things that we cannot change and the ability to know the difference. That's an important key because there are many things that will happen in life that we do not have the power to change; the power is out of our control. There are good things that happen to bad people, and bad things that happen to good people. This is just the ebb and flow of life. But the decision that needs to be made is: how are we going to handle these ebbs and flows, these ups and downs, these goods and bads?

What is in your life right now that is not up to par, that's not bringing you life and peace but is a constant state of anguish and pain? As you embark on the stages of grief, acceptance is a gradual evolution through the process. Initially, you are in a state of shock, and then you enter denial. At the denial stage, a small amount of acceptance starts to break through. You know that you have really started the acceptance process when you get to the stage of anger, because the anger symbolizes that you have left the phase of disbelief or denial. The anger is because you see how senseless and idiotic this event was that interfered with your life, the mistreatment, and how you didn't deserve this, and how on the basis that you are angry, it shows some level of acceptance to the conditions. Bargaining is just a deeper level of acceptance. Full acceptance comes when you are fully willing to surrender everything and to no longer make up excuses for what has happened.

It's the coming to grips with the things in our lives that we know we can't change. Acceptance is freedom. When you follow that train of thought—that we are connected emotionally to someone or something and it is no longer a fit in your life—acceptance allows us to stop all of the continual suffering. It's like a quote I read that said, "Pain is an inevitable part of life, but suffering is optional." If you are reading this book, you probably need to accept that your past relationship is over, and that is time for you to start reevaluating your life and figuring out what are your next ordered steps. If you are like me, this was an extremely difficult decision for me, because I was in a relationship with my past spouse for 30 years. To find out about the betrayals, deceptions, and all of them manipulation, it was evident to me that we couldn't come back from this. At this point of finding out about the betrayals, and even now, about 20 months after the divorce, I don't trust anything that my past relationship has to say. Why? Because of all the lying for years and being made to look like a fool, because the individual she was with knew who I was, they knew everything about me, but I didn't know anything about them.

When you accept the fact that cheating or having adulterous affairs was just part of the fact, also that it was being revealed to you that your past spouse and you are not aligned vibrationally, emotionally, mentally, or physically. My grandfather would often say that two people can't walk together unless they are in agreement, and the fact that they betrayed you to this degree shows that you two were no longer in agreement at all.

"Happiness can be found in the acceptance of what is unknown."

"The more you accept yourself the more you can accept others."

"Acceptance is the first step to healing."

One important key to acceptance is that it will no longer allow you to paint a false image of who you think someone is. You will be required to strip that false image of them out of your mind. It's where the self-lying and self-betrayal stop. Say this quote with me out loud or to yourself, depending on your environment: *"I freely release everything that is no longer a vibrational match and that no longer resonates with me for my highest and best benefit."* Say that to yourself five times.

Another part of acceptance that is important is that you will go through a stage of learning to accept yourself again. Because many times, relationships lead to giving so much of yourself to others that you get lost in the process. A sign that you are beginning to accept the termination of that relationship is that you stop taking calls, stop all forms of communication, stop watching your social media, and stop interacting with them unless there are children involved. You cut off any forms of communication because at this point, it's time for you to start focusing on yourself. The only conversations that you should have are those for exchanging information that has to be exchanged. When you are really ready to move on, you will remove them completely from your life. Of course, this will be a process depending on the number of years, decades, or months you were with this person and the memories that were built throughout that time. But if they were unfaithful throughout the process when you were together, the events and the memories that you have are tainted memories based upon untruth, because they were living a double life.

When you are shown that someone doesn't love you, respect you, support you, or believe in you, that's great information to know. Now you can start taking care of yourself like you used to take care of them. Another area that will show up is family accepting what has happened. If you are from a large family and people look at you as a success, they will have questions, and there will be a lot of talk going on, and speculation; if it's a toxic family like mine, people will pick signs, have opinions, and have a lot to say without having all of the information, where you actually could make an intelligent decision. Some individuals are messy and they need to be in the mix of anything that is happening in others' lives.

The word of encouragement that I have for you is that as you go through this healing journey, you are the first to go through. By going through, you are the changemaker, you are the breaker of curses for generations in your family. By standing in the gap, keeping the faith, standing and healing, and raising your vibration, you are creating a new pattern for your family and your generations. You will stand in spite of fear, you will speak and not weaver, and you will pray. I appreciate every single one of you with all my heart, all my soul, and all my mind. I pray God's abundance of peace, joy, and prosperity upon your life.

As I often say to end my videos on social media, I believe in every single one of you. But you have to believe in yourself. Why I can believe in you? It's because what you are going through and where you are, I was there. I know what the pain feels like. I know what it feels like to be all alone, I know what it feels like to cry out, pray, beg, and ask God to release the pain from your heart. I know it is not to want to accept the things that I was seeing concerning my ex-spouse, because I just did not believe that she was capable of doing these things. We were religious people; she confessed her love for God, she was in church every week, she told me how much she loved me, how handsome she thought I was, all these other things she said, how much of a support she was, and of course we found out that all of this was untrue. But by time I accepted it, I had already been 25 years in a relationship that I knew that was over.

When we can accept the things we cannot change, it will stop all the suffering. It would allow us to experience the peace, joy, and abundance which is promised to us.

If you need support from an exclusive healing community, hit the link and sign in under Healing Heart Community:

www.skool.com/healing-hearts-community-3442

9. BONUS CHAPTER

*H*aving sight but not seeing, having ears to hear but not hearing. I can remember reading a quote which stated that many individuals have sight but black vision. A person without a vision—the visual insight to perceive the things that are possible for them—if you lack that, you will be met with times of extreme discouragement or times when you want to quit. Your vision will take you places that your thoughts alone could never take you. You must write the vision, and it must be plain in design and clear, which will eliminate all of the confusion and worry, because you are fully aware that you can only do what you are capable of—nothing more, nothing less.

Write out the vision for your life. Write it out in present tense, like, "I am grateful and thankful that I'm happily married to the woman of my dreams." What goes hand in hand with your vision is your mindset. Your mindset must represent how you are thinking and what is the prevalent thought on your mind, because from the abundance of your thoughts, we speak. Whatsoever we put in our gates irrigates our mouth gates. You will have a thought, which will cause you to think, which will also call speech, and then some form of action will proceed from all of that.

So, it's critical to read good books—spiritual books and positive books—to help you grow, evolve, and change your life. What music do you frequently listen to? What is the message in the music? Is the message what would be an idea scenario in your life? Who are your closest friends? What are your conversations? What are your mutual interests? Everything in your life, as you move through this healing process, is either helping you get closer to your greatness or is tearing you down.

Something that I would often listen on days when I felt discouraged or overwhelmed throughout my healing process; there are high-frequency vibration music on YouTube, which is free. It is usually longer, extended-form videos for three, four, or five hours. It's something that you can listen to in the background while you clean your house, wash your car, just any number of things that you're doing and what it's going to do is, without you consciously thinking about it, it's going to keep you in a more positive state.

In closing, again, like I've said in the past, I believe in you, but you have to believe in yourself. I know that you can do this because I've done this. What I've written about in this book has been my life for the last 21 months, and I'm sharing this information with you to help you get on the other side, to the place of freedom.

Take the time to write out what is your vision for your healing journey. This might be the last chapter, but it's one of the most important chapters, as well as the chapter on anger. I'm wishing you godspeed and much success in every endeavor. To stay in contact with us, you can follow the link for our private, exclusive, healing community. I just started this awesome group.

www.skool.com/healing-hearts-community-3442

10. FORGIVENESS

The first step, and the most critical, towards your journey of forgiveness, I would suggest that, you take the time to write out an extensive list of all of the things that you perceive that were done against you: all of the injustices, all of the things that caused you pain, and that brought hurt and suffering.

As an example, I'll give you 17 things as part of a list to show you the importance of what you need to put on your list:

1. Adultery
2. Lies
3. Mental manipulation
4. Poisoning me through my food and drinks
5. Slandering my name, as well the name of my family and of our church
6. Destroying my finances my credit
7. Betraying my trust and love
8. Rewarding me evil for purity of my heart
9. Lying and setting up my family
10. Using my trust and naivety against me

11. Never really allowing me to experience love from a spouse
12. Turning our sons, our mutual friends, coworkers, and associates against me unjustly through lies, deceit, and a smear campaign
13. stealing money that I was trying to provide for our family's future. She stole it, used it, and stored it elsewhere, which at this point, I'm not even sure where it is
14. Having an ongoing affair with someone, which showed me our family dynamic was just a lie
15. Taking me for granted—a person that intensely used me because she didn't think I was good enough for her
16. Causing me to feel isolated because I was all alone and not around anyone due to all the hate and venom that was soon towards me
17. Playing constant mind games and lying continually, which I found out later; she was a master manipulator
18. Being completely deceptive in all that she did, pretending to be a wife, a woman of God, someone committed to a relationship, a faithful mother, and a good spouse—all of those things ended up being manifested as just nothing but a lie.

The thing that's most important about forgiveness is that the individual that brought the hurt, pain, suffering, and betrayals into your life may never ever come to you and ask you to forgive them. Forgiveness is holding on to the feelings in the past, so it represents that we can't live in the present or the future healthy. This is why I surrender my heart and I forgive Lisa. I don't need to get an apology or an explanation from her; I only need and I'm ready to move on completely and not have any care or feeling about what's going on in her life.

All of the events that took place are not fair; of course it's very much unjust; it's painful, and definitely it was unnecessary but it was actually necessary for me to see parts of me that needed to change. I learned what it was to set healthy boundaries, to be able to say no, and to love myself. Part of the forgiving process is: Have you forgiven yourself for falling for these tricks and traps?

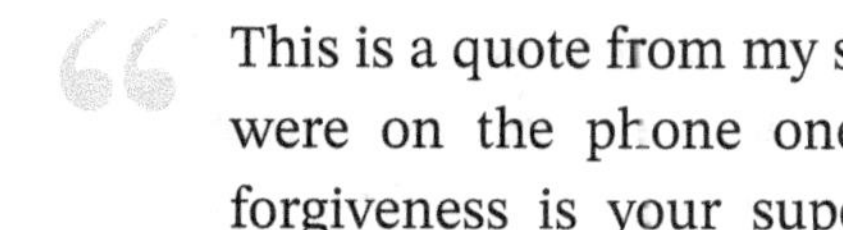

> This is a quote from my sister Kim from Tennessee. We were on the phone one day and she said, "Austin, forgiveness is your superpower." So, I'm telling you today, like she told me, that the forgiveness, the ability to forgive is your superpower.

Seven things I learned about myself that helped myself to bring some sense of balance to this topic of forgiveness. It's easy many times to look at what someone else has done to us, but through this process, there are many signs and symbols that are given us to verify whom we are actually dealing with.

1. I chose her. When I met her, I was dating numerous other women at the same time because I was single, and because she started attending my dad's church, I felt like she was the best choice based on that. So, this was my choice.
2. I dated and married her.
3. I believed that she wanted to have a family and that it would make her happy because based on her words, that's what she said that it was all she wanted.
4. I denied what I was feeling in my body many times throughout our relationship.
5. I ignored my intuition because I believed what she was saying was true.
6. Not only did I lie to myself, but I also bought into believing certain things.
7. I ignored her actions and chose her enticing words and

the image of what I believed that she was, instead of
seeing who she was and what she was.

Forgiveness is a common theme in many holy books. We are
taught that it is beneficial to forgive those who have mistreated us. It
frees us it allows us to release the pain and anguish that someone
has brought to our lives. But what does forgiveness mean? Many
individuals you meet have different opinions on it, and some will say
that if you forgive, that doesn't mean that you need to forget. There
are a lot of coined sayings individuals have concerning forgiveness.
This is a challenging topic because it requires a humility that goes
beyond how hurt you are and how you feel.

Definition of Forgiveness:

Forgiveness is the conscious decision to let go of feelings of
resentment, anger, or vengeance towards someone who has wronged
or hurt you. It involves a transformation of emotional responses and
can lead to personal healing and growth. Forgiveness does not necessarily mean condoning the wrongdoing or restoring the relationship
to its previous state; rather, it is about releasing the burden of negative emotions to foster peace and move forward.

Can you actually pray for someone that has done wrong to you? I
know that I'm in the energy of forgiveness when I can pray for them,
regardless of what they have done to me. The prayer for them is self-
ish, if I'm being honest, but it's also life-transforming. The prayer is
that they would open their eyes and see all the things they are doing
and that they would turn their hearts to the Most High and seek
forgiveness. Because it's not God's will that anyone with perish, but
that they would turn their hearts to Him and seek forgiveness and
pray.

The prayer must be felt in your heart. Feel it, acknowledge it, and
then release it. You must be keenly aware to discard any thought that
comes into your mind concerning arguing with them or speaking to

them about what they have done. I often know that I haven't forgiven because I catch myself having an argument with them while I'm alone in my vehicle or in my home, but the argument is as if they are standing in front of me which is a sign that there is unforgiveness that needs to be dealt with.

Let go of the pain. Why would you hold on to it when you can just release it? Let it go. Now you releasing the pain is not a sign that nothing has happened in the past or that you weren't violated in some way. It just means that you have decided that you no longer want to be in alignment, vibration, and energy with the pain; instead, you are releasing and letting go of the pain.

Give it up. Surrender it. Yield. Allow yourself to experience the goodness of life and all of its abundance. Allowing yourself to forgive someone isn't an indictment on yourself; but it's actually a freeing of yourself from the things that were done against you. As long as you hold on to what they did, you cannot allow your heart to completely heal so that you can manifest the things that you actually want.

Also, the reason I suggest that you write out that list that we discussed at the beginning of this chapter is so that you can take a look at what they did or what you perceived they did, what you are holding on to, and what you are excited about moving away from; the freedom to no longer hold on to and ask for a deed that is from your past. But when it's not addressed, It lives rent-free in your present reality and future until you decide that enough is enough.

If you allow the actions, behaviors, and deeds of someone else to affect you, that means that they are controlling you. They have these imaginary strings like a puppet master that they are pulling them, which affects your life, attitude, mindset, actions and behavior. Why would you, as a mature grown adult, allow someone else to control you, and on top of it, you have given them your permission unknowingly? It is time to set yourself free. Whom God sets free is free indeed. You can take your power back by deciding that "I am willing and able to forgive them of what they have done."

> "Resentment is like drinking poison and then hoping it will kill your enemy."
>
> — NELSON MANDELA

> "To forgive is to set prisoners free and discover that the prisoner was you."
>
> — LEWIS B SMEDES

> "Holding on to anger is like grasping a hot coal with the intent of throwing it at someone else, and you end up being the one that gets hurt, because you are holding on to it."
>
> — BUDDHA

In writing this part of the book, I came across a true story of forgiveness that I know will make a tremendous difference in your life. The story is about a shooting that took place in Pennsylvania at West Nickel Mines School, which was a one-room Amish classroom. The attacker, Charles Carl Roberts IV, took hostages and shot ten girls, ages 6 to 13, killing six—five in the initial incident one later from complications in 2024. To add insult to injury, after holding those little girls hostage and killing six of them, he took his own life.

Through that difficult process, which I can imagine as a father—but I'm a father that has three sons which I love—but as a man having a daughter in some senseless act of violence was perpetrated against her, because whatever his reason was, would have been a very difficult pill to swallow. But the Amish community joined together in unity to heal and to forgive from this. It was a visible testament that they sent support to his family, attended his funeral, and displayed many attributes that exemplified what they have read in their Bibles and evidently lived out in their lives.

Nobody said forgiveness would be easy—it's simple but not easy. It's the ability to let go of that hot coal, to release that senseless, devious deed, and to emotionally no longer surrender your energy to the traumatic event that happened to you. Just because it happened to you, it doesn't mean that it is defines you—unless you refuse to let it go. Heart-centered meditations with prayer of release are part of the catalyst of getting free.

Number one key that I often go back to and reflect on is I learned from personal experience that I can actually pray for the person that did the wrong to me. From a place of not praying for their demise or destruction, but praying about myself, how I feel emotionally about what has happened, and that I have a pure heart that isn't riddled with anger, bitterness, resentment, and unforgiveness.

In closing, I say,

"Forgiveness is simple, but it's also challenging at the same time."

— ARNOLD AUSTIN, COACH AJ

https://www.youtube.com/channel/UCBHsTrBoLNDIzbEh8o TtVeg

ABOUT THE AUTHOR

Arnold Austin is a certified relationship trauma coach through the esteemed John Maxwell. He has over 25 years of biblical studies under his belt and has launched and built numerous successful businesses. He is the father of 3 sons. Through the coaching his goal is to help to train and teach individuals how to heal themselves and in the process that they would discover their purpose and fulfill their destiny.